Nab the Crab

amicus readers

Mankato, Minnesota

by Marie Powell

Ideas for Parents and Teachers

Amicus Readers let children practice reading informational texts at the earliest reading levels. Familiar words and concepts with close photo-text matches support early readers.

Before Reading
- Discuss the cover photo with the child. What does it tell him?
- Ask the child to predict what she will learn in the book.

Read the Book
- "Walk" through the book and look at the photos. Let the child ask questions.
- Read the book to the child, or have the child read independently.

After Reading
- Use the word family list at the end of the book to review the text.
- Prompt the child to make connections. Ask: *What other words end with -ab?*

Amicus Readers are published by Amicus
P.O. Box 1329, Mankato, MN 56002
www.amicuspublishing.us

Library of Congress Cataloging-in-Publication Data

Powell, Marie, 1958-
  Nab the crab / Marie Powell.
      pages cm. -- (Word families)
  ISBN 978-1-60753-513-3 (hardcover) -- ISBN 978-1-60753-544-7 (eBook)
  1. English language--Phonetics--Juvenile literature.
2. English language--Rhyme--Juvenile literature. 3. Vocabulary--Juvenile literature. I. Title.
  PE1135.P64 2013
  428.6--dc23
                              2013006856

Photo Credits: Kim Reinick/Shutterstock Images, cover; EcoPrint/Shutterstock Images, 1; Thinkstock, 3; Volodymyr Krasyuk/Shutterstock Images, 5; Shutterstock Images, 6, 7; Patrick Bigatel/Shutterstock Images, 9; Paul Vinten/Shutterstock Images, 11; Ivan Kuzmin/Shutterstock Images, 12; Chris Burt/Shutterstock Images, 15

Produced for Amicus by The Peterson Publishing Company and Red Line Editorial.

Editor Jenna Gleisner
Designer Marie Tupy
Printed in the United States of America
Mankato, MN
July, 2013
PA 1938
10 9 8 7 6 5 4 3 2 1

A **crab** hides under a **slab** of rock. A hungry bird looks for it.

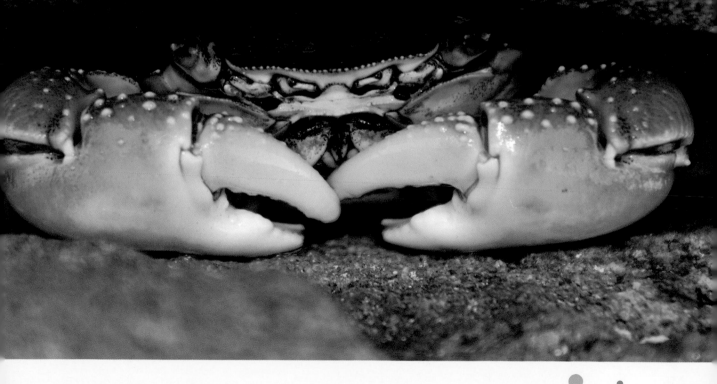

A **crab** has ten legs. The front legs are pincers that help it **grab** food.

A **crab** walks sideways.
It likes to **jab** and dig
in the sand.

Birds try to **stab** a **crab** with their beaks. The **crab** has a hard shell to keep it safe.

A **crab** can hide in its shell. Some **crab** shells look **drab**, like a rock.

A **crab** lifts up its pincers.

If it pinches the bird,

it might leave a **scab**!

The **crab** crawls back under the **slab** of rock. Will the bird try to **nab** the **crab** again?

Word Family: -ab

Word families are groups of words
that rhyme and are spelled the same.

Here are the **-ab** words in this book:

crab
drab
grab
jab
nab
scab
slab
stab

Can you spell any other words
with **-ab**?